Detroit
PISTONS

BY JIM GIGLIOTTI

Published by The Child's World®
1980 Lookout Drive • Mankato, MN 56003-1705
800-599-READ • www.childsworld.com

ISBN 9781503824522
LCCN 2018964276

Printed in the United States of America
PA02416

ABOUT THE AUTHOR

Jim Gigliotti has worked for the University
of Southern California's athletic department,
the Los Angeles Dodgers, and the National
Football League. He is now an author who
has written more than 100 books, mostly
for young readers, on a variety of topics.

TABLE OF

CONTENTS

Go, Pistons! 4

Who Are the Pistons? 7

Where They Came From 8

Who They Play 11

Where They Play 12

The Basketball Court 15

Good Times 16

Tough Times 19

All the Right Moves 20

Heroes Then 23

Heroes Now 24

What They Wear 27

Team Stats 28

Glossary 30

Find Out More 31

Index 32

GO, PISTONS!

The Detroit Pistons have a long history. They have had many great players and coaches. They have had winning teams, too. The Pistons have won three NBA titles. Only five teams have more. It has been a while since the team has been on top, though. Detroit's last title was in 2004. Their fans hope the next one will come soon.

The arrival of Blake Griffin in 2018 gave the Pistons a key player to build a team around.

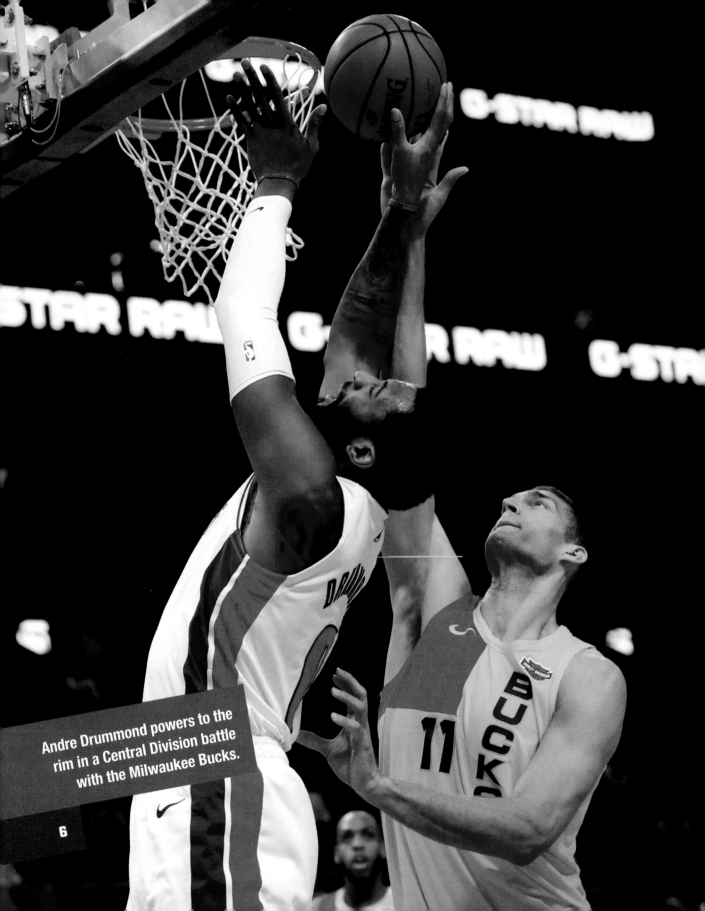

Andre Drummond powers to the rim in a Central Division battle with the Milwaukee Bucks.

WHO ARE THE PISTONS?

The Pistons play in the NBA Central Division. That division is part of the Eastern Conference. The other teams in the Central Division are the Chicago Bulls, the Cleveland Cavaliers, the Indiana Pacers, and the Milwaukee Bucks. The Pistons have finished in first place 11 times. They have made it to the **NBA Finals** seven times.

WHERE THEY CAME FROM

The Pistons began playing in Fort Wayne, Indiana, in 1941. The team was part of the first NBA season in 1950. The team got its name because the owner was in the car business. Pistons are important parts of a car engine. In the 1958 season, the team moved to Detroit. The team name was still perfect. Many cars were made in Detroit.

Until 1957, the team was the Fort Wayne Zollner Pistons. That was the name of the company that owned the team.

Glenn Robinson rises up to shoot over a Chicago Bulls player in an Eastern Conference matchup.

WHO THEY PLAY

The Pistons play 82 games each season. They play 41 games at home and 41 on the road. They play four games against each of the other Central Division teams. They play 36 games against other Eastern Conference teams. Finally, the Pistons play each of the teams in the Western Conference twice. That's a lot of basketball! Each June, the winners of the Western and Eastern Conferences play each other in the NBA Finals.

WHERE THEY PLAY

The Pistons have played in many different **arenas**. The first was a high school gym in Fort Wayne. Basketball wasn't nearly as popular then as it is now! For many years the Pistons played at The Palace outside of Detroit. In the 2018 season, the team moved into Little Caesars Arena. It is named for a pizza company in Detroit.

Why is the Pistons mascot Hooper a horse? Because pistons create horsepower in engines!

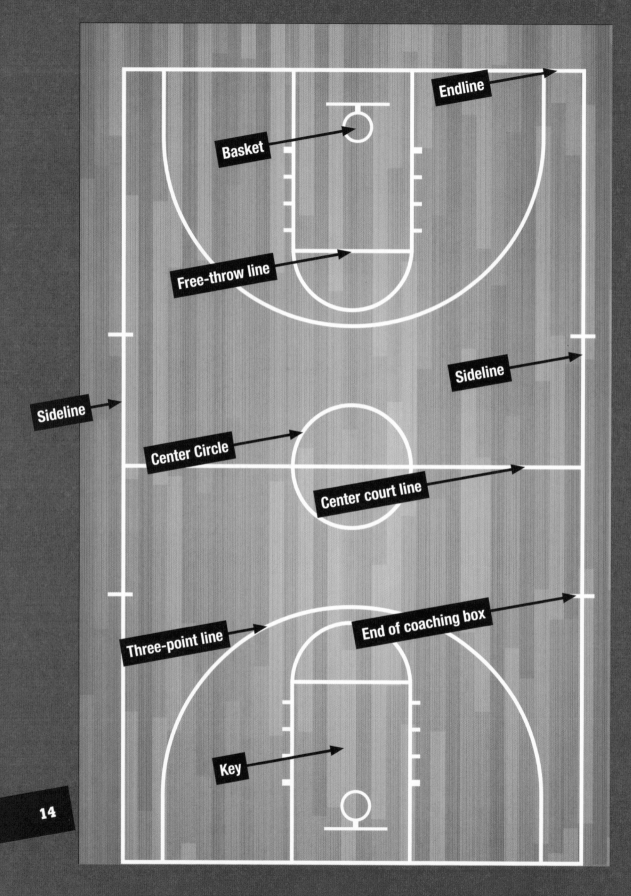

Endline

Basket

Free-throw line

Sideline

Sideline

Center Circle

Center court line

Three-point line

End of coaching box

Key

THE BASKETBALL COURT

An NBA court is 94 feet long and 50 feet wide (28.6 m by 15.24 m). Nearly all the courts are made from hard maple wood. Rubber mats under the wood help make the floor springy. Each team paints the court with its **logo** and colors. Lines on the court show the players where to take shots. The diagram on the left shows the important parts of the NBA court.

The Pistons' home arena is in downtown Detroit. It is connected to offices and shops, so people can walk to the game from work!

GOOD TIMES

The Pistons have made the **playoffs** 41 times. The team made the playoffs each of its first 14 years in the NBA. Its first title didn't come until 1989. It wasn't long until the second. The Pistons won again in 1990. The Pistons made the playoffs eight years in a row starting in 2002. They won 64 games in 2006. That is their most ever.

Detroit's Dennis Rodman battles the Lakers during the 1989 NBA Finals.

17

Forward Grant Hill shows off the unpopular jersey color the Pistons wore in the 1990s.

TOUGH TIMES

The Pistons didn't win a playoff series from 1992 through 2001. The fans were unhappy. The team changed its colors during that time. It went from blue and red to teal. The fans were really unhappy about that. The team changed back. The worst time came in 2005. The team got into a fight with the Pacers. It was called The Palace Brawl.

ALL THE RIGHT MOVES

Tayshaun Prince made "The Block" to save a playoff game against Indiana in 2004. Bill Laimbeer and Dennis Rodman also made their best moves on defense. They helped give the Pistons the nickname "Bad Boys." Big **center** Andre Drummond is the team's latest star on defense. He makes it tough on opponents around the basket.

In basketball, players can block shots using their hands. If they hit or touch the shooter, a foul can be called.

Go ahead, try to get past big Andre Drummond. He can score, but his biggest help to the Pistons comes on defense.

Hall of Famer Isiah Thomas was named to 12 All-Star teams while with Detroit.

HEROES THEN

Former Pistons star Dave Bing was so popular he became mayor of Detroit. Bob Lanier was so big he wore a size 22 shoe. Isiah Thomas and Joe Dumars were all-stars. They helped carry the Pistons to the top in the late 1980s and early 1990s. Vinnie Johnson had a cool nickname. He was called "The Microwave." That is because he could be a hot shooter!

The Pistons traded for Blake Griffin in 2018. That big man is a big scorer. Andre Drummond also was a good scorer in 2018. He was the league's top rebounder, too. That was a hint of what was to come. He had some monster games in 2019. Reggie Jackson is a talented **guard**. When he is playing well, he can fill up the basket. (That means score a lot of points!)

Blake Griffin is almost impossible to stop near the basket. He is one of the NBA's best dunkers.

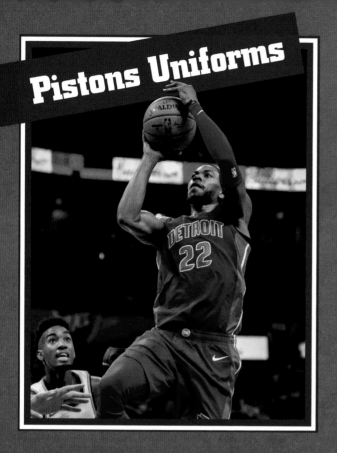

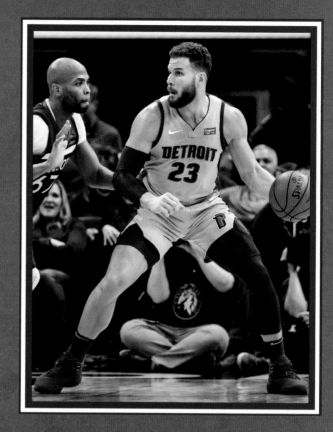

WHAT THEY WEAR

NBA players wear a **tank top** jersey. Players wear team shorts. Each player can choose his own sneakers. Some players also wear knee pads or wrist guards.

Each NBA team has more than one jersey style. The pictures at left show some of the Pistons' jerseys.

The NBA basketball is 29.5 inches (75 cm) around. It is covered with leather. The leather has small bumps called pebbles.

The pebbles on a basketball help players grip it.

TEAM STATS

Here are some of the all-time career records for the Detroit Pistons. These stats are complete through all of the 2018–19 NBA regular season.

GAMES

Joe Dumars	1,018
Isiah Thomas	979

REBOUNDS PER GAME

Andre Drummond	13.4
Bailey Howell	11.8

ASSISTS PER GAME

Kevin Porter	10.1
Isiah Thomas	9.3

FREE-THROW PCT.

Chauncey Billups	.892
Ben Gordon	.857

STEALS PER GAME

M.L. Carr	2.1
Chris Ford	1.9

THREE-POINT FIELD GOALS

Joe Dumars	990
Chauncey Billups	890

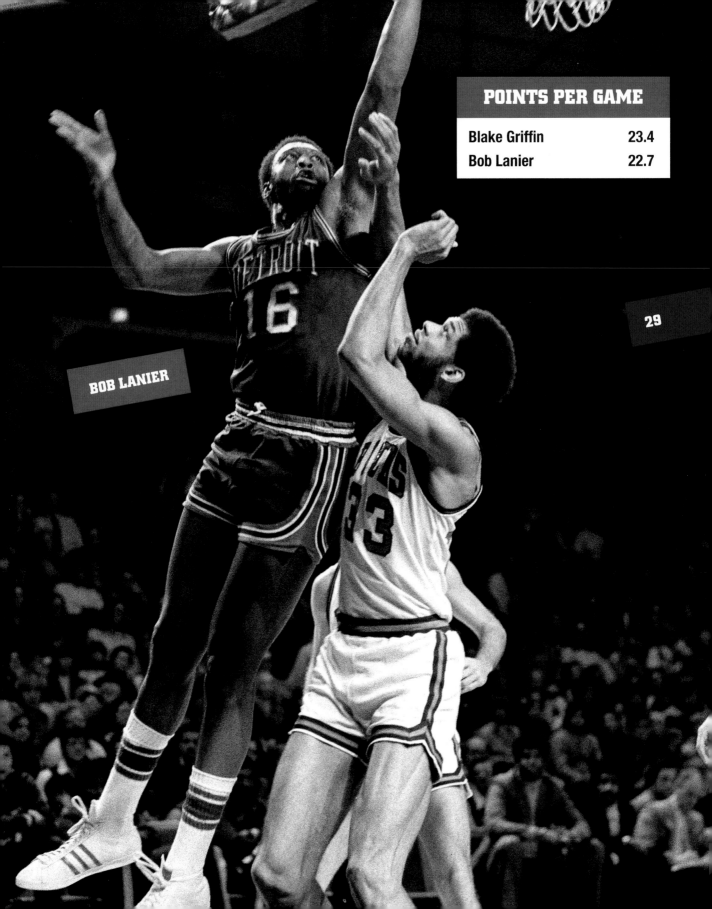

POINTS PER GAME

Blake Griffin	23.4
Bob Lanier	22.7

29

BOB LANIER

arenas *(uh-REE-nuhz)* the buildings in which a basketball team plays its games

center *(SEN-ter)* a basketball position that plays near the basket

guard *(GARD)* a player in basketball who usually dribbles and makes passes

logo *(LOW-go)* a team or company's symbol

NBA Finals *(NBA FINE-ulz)* the championship series for the NBA

playoffs *(PLAY-offs)* games played between top teams to determine who moves ahead

tank top *(TANK TOP)* a style of shirt that has straps over the shoulders and no sleeves

FIND OUT MORE

IN THE LIBRARY

Bryant, Howard. *Legends: The Best Players, Games, and Teams in Basketball.* New York, NY: Philomel Books, 2016.

Schaller, Bob with Coach Dave Harnish. *The Everything Kids' Basketball Book.* Avon, MA: Adams Media, 2017.

Whiting, Jim. *Detroit Pistons.* Mankato, MN: Creative Paperbacks, 2017.

ON THE WEB

Visit our website for links about the Detroit Pistons:

childsworld.com/links

Note to Parents, Teachers, and Librarians: We routinely verify our Web links to make sure they are safe and active sites. So encourage your readers to check them out!

INDEX

Bing, Dave, 23

Central Division, 6, 7, 11

Chicago Bulls, 7, 10

Cleveland Cavaliers, 7

court, 15

Drummond, Andre, 6, 20, 21, 24

Dumars, Joe, 23

Eastern Conference, 7, 10, 11

Fort Wayne, Indiana, 8, 9, 12

Griffin, Blake, 5, 24, 25

Hill, Grant, 18

Hooper, 13

Indiana Pacers, 7, 19

Jackson, Reggie, 24

jerseys, 27

Johnson, Vinnie, 23

Laimbeer, Bill, 20

Lanier, Bob, 23

Little Caesars Arena, 12

Milwaukee Bucks, 6, 7

Prince, Tayshaun, 20

Robinson, Glenn, 10

Rodman, Dennis, 17, 20

The Palace, 12, 19

Thomas, Isiah, 22, 23

Western Conference, 11

Zollner Pistons, 9